Hunger Beyond Domesday

CAROL CARTWRIGHT

For all their help,advice and encouragement
I would like to thank –

Mrs.Mary Anderson
Mr.Michael Blakeway
Dr.Margaret Gelling
Mr.John Hardacre,Curator of Winchester Cathedral
Mrs.Eileen Venables
Mrs.Sue Warrilow,Mrs.Sylvia Laker and Mrs.June
Tubb of the Hungerford Library;

And lastly I would like to thank my family,
Phil,Claire and Daniel,
without whose help this book would not have been
completed.

'Kennedy Map' 1794 by W.Francis.Donated to the
Town and Manor by the Kennedy Family.Reproduced
here by kind permission of the Constable and
Trustees of the Town and Manor of Hungerford.

Andrews & Dury Map 1773,reproduced here by kind
permission of the Wiltshire Archaeological and
Natural History Society.

Memorial to Sir Robert de Hungerford (front cover)
reproduced here by kind permission of the
Reverend Andrew Sawyer,Vicar of St.Lawrence's Church.

ISBN   0-9519506-0-6

PUBLISHED BY CAROL CARTWRIGHT
           53 CHURCH STREET
           HUNGERFORD,Berkshire,RG17 OJH

Printed by Printaquik, Newbury. Tel: 0635 35889 Fax: 0635 37201

Chapter One

Romano-British Beginnings

It has so far been impossible to assign a date to the founding of Hungerford.The absence of any entry under Hungerford in the Domesday Book has led to the assumption that there may not have been any settlement here until after that date.

The name "hunger ford" implies a settlement on poor land at a ford,a place where people go hungry or have starved.This is Ekwall's definition,supported by Gelling(1991),and there are no other early forms suggesting any other derivation.There is no truth in the rumour that Hingwar the Dane drowned in the ford.The name was a meaningful description for inhabitants of West Berkshire,the earliest surviving mention of the name is used as a reference point to locate another place (Eddington 1101-1118). (VCH.Berks.)

The evidence for an earlier existence for Hungerford is sketchy.And yet there are other places known to have existed before 1086 that were not been mentioned in the Domesday Book,for example Hidden in 984 AD.

An archaeological dig undertaken by Thames Valley Archaeological Services (TVAS) on the Charnham Street industrial site has uncovered Bronze Age relics including what appears to be a place of worship,sixth century Saxon remains and medieval dwellings.The Kennet valley has been occupied for over 3000 years and more evidence lies waiting to be unearthed.

Margary's Roman Roads of Britain shows a Roman road running from Wickham to Folly Farm crossroads.All traces of road running nearer towards the Kennet have been ploughed up,but the road appears again running along the crest of the hill through Cake Wood and Hens Wood until it reaches Cunetio near Mildenhall.There must have been a Roman bridge at Eddington and presumably it should be possible to find some traces of it.

Roman sites have been discovered at Kintbury,Tottenham House and Bedwyn Brail,where there is an as yet unexplored 5-acre site.There is also the famous villa and mosaic at Littlecote. The dig there revealed a medieval building with a bake-house alongside the ancient road to Ramsbury which ran on the south side of the Kennet.All that remains of that road today is the public footpath and right of way.These footpaths are often a good indication of an older route.This medieval road may have run on top of the Roman road.No Roman roads have yet been found linking the other sites with the east-west road.But there must have been a network of local roads to serve these sites,and there were also scattered British dwellings.Very little fieldwork has been done as yet.Before the Vokins site at Eddington is developed the opportunity should be taken to look for Roman remains,though they

ROMANO – BRITISH SITES (fig.i)

KEY

///// EARTHWORKS
✝ SITES
—— ROMAN ROADS

WALBURY HILL

700 FEET

ROMAN ROAD TO CUNETIO

ROMAN SITE

WANSDYKE

CHISBURY

BEDWINDAN

ROMAN POTTERY

ROMAN SITE

RIVER KENNET

IKENILDE STRET

700 FEET

RIVER KENNET

BRITISH SETTLE-MENT

ROMAN SITE

800 FEET

BRITISH SETTLEMENT

BRONZE AGE RELICS

BEDWINDAN

4

are perhaps more likely to be found 400 yards upstream where a line continuing the known Roman road would cross.

The Romano-British people were mainly of Celtic stock.The Celts had spread from the Danube valley across Europe.Their launching point for colonising England was Belgium,hence the name Belgae later given to them.Obviously Roman troops and traders intermarried with them.But basically Roman rule was imposed on a subject people from above and it left very few permanent examples of the Roman way of life to be absorbed by the natives.The Celts were warriors and skilled craftsmen with a strong oral history tradition. The Celtic language remained virtually unaltered,just a few loan words came from Latin - "ffenestr" is window in Modern Welsh.

After the fall of the Roman Empire the native population gradually deserted decaying Roman towns and villas.They forgot how to maintain the stone buildings,drains and heating systems.For defence purposes they retired to the Iron Age hillforts,examples of these locally are Chisbury and Walbury Hill.Wallingtons and Walcot (now Wawcot) farm are sites of Romano-British settlements (Gelling,1976).The Old English name for foreigner was "wealas" or "wealsc" (pronounced wealsh),in time this word also came to mean serf or slave.These sites were identified by the incoming Anglo-Saxons as native enclaves.Some Roman roads were still usable and recognised by the Anglo-Saxons and used as reference points in charter boundaries,(Little Bedwyn 778 AD.and Great Bedwyn 968 AD.)though the Anglo-Saxons thought them the work of the British.Hence "weala weg"- welsh way. The Celts called themselves "cymry" which means fellow countrymen,the name also being seen in "Cumbria".The Celtic names for local rivers are the only evidence remaining of pre-Saxon inhabitants of West Berks,the Kennet and the now lost river-name Bedewindan which gave its name to Bedwyn.It means birch white or "bedw gwyn" in Modern Welsh.Today the river is called the Dun which is a back-naming from the mill. (Gelling,1976)

There were Saxons in parts of Britain for almost the whole of the fifth century,invited by local British chiefs to help defend them against the Picts and Danes.Most of these were along the East-Anglian coast to begin with,but the Anglo-Saxons gradually made their way inland,along major rivers like the Thames.

Unlike the Roman invasion which comprised an army and a few settlers, the Anglo-Saxon invasion was a movement of a whole people.Consequently the former inhabitants were swamped and enslaved or they fled. The western side of Britain with its rougher terrain was a natural stronghold.Cumbria and modern Wales were "North Wales" and Cornwall was "West Wales" inhabited by the Corn-welsh. Other Celts fled to Brittany in the fifth and sixth centuries.That ancient link is still evident today as the Breton and Welsh languages are still mutually comprehensible.

From the early fifth century when imperial Rome said it could no
longer defend its extended empire,there was a period of upheaval
all over Europe.This was probably reflected in the Kennet
valley.Not far upstream there was Littlecote which must slowly
have fallen into decay.The precise movements of people in the
fifth and sixth centuries are difficult to determine.But at
Undy's Farm the TVAS team found proof of a sixth century Saxon
hut with post holes for roof supports,as well as pottery
remains.There is also evidence that early medieval arable use of
the land gave way to grassland as the terrain became increasingly
wet.(TVAS Interim Report 1989). What other proof might lie
undiscovered near the Kennet and the Dun?

Chapter Two

Saxon Settlement

The Saxons naturally settled the best land first.They had brought
with them a new heavier plough capable of turning the wetter
earth in the lowland valleys.The sixth century Saxons who left
traces at Undy's Farm were attracted to a good water supply and
the prospect of a better crop than that produced on thin upland
soils.

Settlement names in the Ock valley in NW Berkshire suggest an
early agricultural community there as well.It seems that the
earliest settlements were formed in valleys and named after
topographical features to do with the water supply such as
fords,rivers and dry sites for building.(Gelling,1988)

In the Hungerford district the early sites were Denford, Hidden,
Standen, Ham(m) (river meadow,NOT ham —home), Bedwyn (Celtic
name), Shalbourn(shallow stream), Kintbury(fortified place on the
Kennet),and Inkpen(inge penne,hill enclosure referring to Walbury
hillfort).The name-form "hunger ford" would appear to be a
similar descriptive name connected with the water supply.Was
there a sixth century settlement on poor soil at the ford?Did the
land become too wet for good cultivation?

Charters describing Saxon land holdings in West Berkshire and
East Wiltshire have survived in sufficient numbers for a map to
be drawn (fig.ii).The charter bounds in many cases correspond
very closely with modern parish boundaries.The northern charter
bounds of Collingbourne in 921 mention several of the same
landmarks used to define the Great Bedwyn estate in 968, and the
southernmost bounds of Little Bedwyn from 778 are repeated for
the north side of Great Bedwyn nearly 200 years later.It is
frustrating that no documents relating to the land on which
Hungerford stands have survived.

Noblemen and others in the king's household expected to be
rewarded by grants of land.Strictly speaking the grant did not
convey ownership but rather the right to receive dues and tithes
formerly due to the king.With the exception of military
service,bridge building and the construction of
fortifications,the thegns or noblemen had complete rights over
their land. They now received the "feorm" (Old English for food-
rent)(Latin—"firma") which this land had formerly rendered to the
king.This made little difference to the peasants who now served a
local lord rather than a distant king.The land conveyed by
charter came to be known as "bocland" or bookland,as it was all
drawn up in a book or charter.The new owner had the freedom to
sell or bequeathe it as he wished.This freedom often meant there
was an opportunity to found a monastery there that would be free
of the burden of food-rents and royal services."Folcland" or
folkland from which the king drew his feorm and customary

ANGLO-SAXON
ESTATES IN THE
TENTH CENTURY
(fig ii)

From charter evidence.

C.S. Charters can be found
in the Cartularium Saxonicum.

C.S.	Date
225	778 AD
324	803·5
508	863
611	904
635	921
677	931
678	931
699	933
748	940
1067	961
1079	961
1213	968

Map labels:

LAMBURNINGA BOUNDARY
HYDD CS.1079
ÆTHELINGADENE
DENFORDA CS.678
CYNETAN
BYRIG CS.678
HAMSTEDE 961 AD.
INGE STREAM
INGE PENNE CS.678
HREMNESBYRIG
RIVER KENNET
FORSCANFELD CS.324
FROXAFELDA 968 AD
BEDEWINDA
BEDEWINDE CS.225
SHALBOURNE STREAM
HAMME CS.677
BUTERMERE AESCMERE CS.508
SCEALDEBORNAN CS.611
STOCE CS.611
BEDEWINDE CS.1213
CRAFFT CS.678
MILDANHALD CS.324
FOREST OF SAFERNOC CS.699
BYRBEC CS.1067
WDUTUN CS.718
COLLINGABURNAN CS.635
PEVESIGE CS.748

services was the ordinary land held by a ceorl and his family,or
land that a nobleman owned without the benefit of charter.King
Ine's (d.726)laws included passages covering the tenancy
agreements that might be made between a noble and an individual
peasant.(Stenton)

This individual was still a free man and,subject to certain
conditions like leaving the land in good order before leaving his
lord's service,he "could go where he would".This phrase is often
seen in the Domesday Book.The size of a Saxon land- holding
varied enormously from the ealdormen with hundreds of acres to a
man with 30 acres or less.In good times it was possible to save
money to buy more land,the aim was to own five hides(1 hide =
c.120 acres) and a church and be counted as a thegn.However in
bad times a man could not support his family and this led to the
formation of the many villages called Charlton in southern
England.The word comes from ceorl -a freeman and tun   -
farm.Cerleton by Hungerford was probably formed when a group of
families pooled their resources to try to offset the effects of a
dreadful harvest perhaps coupled with higher taxes to fund a
war.The alternative was to trade one's freedom for security in a
lord's service.Today Charlton is rather better known as Freeman's
Marsh,Hopgrass Farm and Charnham Street.

The earlier estates had topographical names,if named at all. It
was only in the late tenth century that manors came to be called
after a prominent owner,formed with the personal name and 'tun'
or 'ham',farm or home,eg.Leverton,Chilton,Avington, Eddington
(Gelling,1988)).A 984 charter from King Aethelred to Brihtric for
a local estate,which was then unnamed,has survived.-

Aerest on Cynetan aet Scoellas ealdcotan;thaet up andlang
First on the Kennet at Scoella's old cottage up along

streames oth Eadgife gemaere;swa north innan Hydene;thanon
the stream to Edgiva's boundary,so north into Hidden thence

north on lamburninga mearce;swa est andlang mearce oth
north to the Lambourn boundary,so east along the boundary to

aelfwiges gemaere;swa suth andlang gemaeres on Hyddene;
Aelfwige's boundary,so south along the boundary to Hidden,

swa suth be gemaere that eft innan Cynetan strem.
so south by the boundary that ends in the Kennet stream.
                              Thirteenth century version.

The charter bounds always run clockwise and can be followed on a
modern map,where they seem to correspond with the modern parish
boundary.Scoella's cottage was old then in 984.Might its shadow
have survived to Domesday Book's Colecote and subsequently till
1894 as Calcot?Edgiva's boundary is to the west of the estate(it
later became Chilton -estate of the young nobleman) and so cannot
be Eddington.If it were Eddington then the plot described above

would have to have been Denford,and as such would have been called by name as Denford was in common usage by 931.Aelfwige's boundary is to the east of the bounds and might well be referring to land granted to Aelfric in 961,this plot is now Eddington.By elimination the bounds studied above are Leverton.Leofwaru who gave the estate her name,must have been a later owner than Brihtric.

Almost all the early Anglo-Saxon charters that have survived have been collected in the Cartularium Saxonicum by Walter de Gray Birch,published 1885-1893.Each one has a reference number eg. CS.225.This particular number refers to the oldest surviving West Saxon charter dating from 778.King Cynewulf of the West Saxons granted a large estate at Little Bedwyn to Earl Bica.The bounds of that estate as well as Great Bedwyn and Burbage are examined by O.G.S.Crawford in the Wiltshire Archaeological Magazine.It is evidence like this that has enabled the map (fig.ii) to be drawn up.Another charter that has especial relevance for this area is CS.677.

This was a grant of land by King Aethelstan in 931 to one of his thegns Wulfgar.The estate was Ham,and some of its original outline can be noted in field edges on a large scale O.S. map.Attached to the charter is Wulfgar's will.This document,CS 678,is immensely valuable and can shed much light on this district and is therefore reproduced here in full.

Wulfgar's Will 931 AD.

I.Wulfgar,give the land at Collingbourn,after my day,to Aeffe for her day;and let her till it for the common need of both our souls,and during three days,supply with food the servants of God where my body may rest,on the commemoration day;and give to the mass-priest five pence,and to each of the others two;and after her day,to Winchester,to the New Monastery,for my soul,to have and to enjoy,and not to be given from the monastery.And I give the land at Inkpen,after my day,to Aeffe to enjoy and to administer;and let her have every year,at the vill,of all the yearly produce the three parts ,and the fourth (be given)to God's servants at Kintbury,for my soul, and for my fathers,and for my grandfathers.Then,after her day,(let it be given) to the holy place at Kintbury,for my,Wulfgar's,soul,who give it,and for Wulfric's and for Wulfhere's who first acquired it,to have and to enjoy,and never to alienate.Then I give the land at Crofton,after my day,to Wynsige and Aelfsige,and all which I thereon get.And I give the land at Denford,after my day,to Aethelstan and Kynestan,if they until then duly obey me.And I give the land at Buttermere after my day,to Byrhtsige,2 hides;and to Ceolstan's sons one,if they until then duly obey me.And I bequeath,in words,Ashmere to such of my young kinsmen who shall best obey me. And I will that Aeffe supply provisions,from the three parts at Inkpen, to the servants of God at Kintbury, three days in twelve

months,one day for me,the second for my father,the third for my
grandfather.
And I give the land at Ham to Aeffe,after my day;and let her till
thereon,for the soul's need of both,and at Easter, supply with
provisions for three days,the servants of God where my body may
rest;and after her day to Winchester to the Old Monastery of the
Holy Trinity,to have and to enjoy and never to alienate.
Here is made known that Wulfgar gave Ham to the Old Monastery
after the day of Aeffe his wife.

(Trans. Thorpe)

It is interesting to note that Inkpen was given to the servants
of God at Kintbury after Aeffe's death.In 1086 Amesbury Abbey is
listed as the principal owner of Kintbury. Was this an instance
where bookland had been granted to a religious foundation?The
charter granting Inkpen to Wulfgar's grandfather Wulfhere has not
survived,so it is not certain. However in 1086 Inkpen is shown as
having been two manors held by two thegns in freehold from King
Edward.Did the abbey sell or lease the land,or exchange it for
more profitable or more conveniently situated manors?Either is
possible.

The size of Wulfgar's holding at Inkpen is not clear.However his
estate at Collingbourn is thought to have included both Kingston
and Ducis when granted to him in 921,which is an impressive
size.Grandfather Wulfhere was an Earldorman,an early predecessor
of the title Earl,and possibly a kinsman of the king,and
therefore perhaps likely to have received an equally generous
estate at Inkpen.He was also granted Buttermere at that time —
863.These great Earls held sway over huge tracts of land that
often took their name from the river on whose banks they were
founded.Similarly Bedwyn,Kintbury, Lambourn and Shalbourn which
all began as royal manors had been,by 1086,divided into 5 or more
smaller manors and granted away.

Inkpen could have been a similar estate which included all the
land between the Shalbourn stream and the Kintbury boundary,south
of the Kennet to the hills.It may have been divided up by the
Abbess of Amesbury into convenient plots for sale or
exchange.Certainly by the time of the Domesday survey Inkpen had
been subdivided and re-organised.
      Inkpen itself —two manors into one
      Inglewood i   —two manors into one
      Inglewood ii —two manors into one
      Inglewood iii —four separate holders from a thegn
          called William.
Here are ten pre-conquest settlements which in the 150 years
between Wulfgar's death and the Domesday survey have twice been
re-organised.The coincidence of the names lends force to the
argument that local men would have seen them as having been many
parts of a single entity.One of these manors could have been
Hungerford.There are instances of scattered villages being
treated by their lord as a single manor for administrative
purposes and appearing thus in the Domesday Book.(Stenton,Anglo-
Saxon England p481)

Saxon Kings

WODEN — BAELDAEG — BROND — FRITHOGAR

FREAWINE — WIG — GEWIS — ESLA — ELESA

CERDIC

CREODA

CYNRIC

CEOLWULF — CUTHA — CEAWLIN 560-592

CUTHGILS — CEOLWULF 592 — CEOL 592-597 — CUTHWINE

CENFRITH — CYNEGILS 611-642 — CUTHA | CADDA

CENFUS — CWICHELM CENWALH 672 — CEOLWALD | CYNEGILS | COENBERHT

AESCWINE 674-676 — CUTHRED — CENRED — CENTWINE 676 — CADWALLA 680-688

INE 688-726 — INGELD d 718

AETHELHEARD 728-741 — EOPPA

CUTHRED 741-756 — SIGEBERHT — CYNEWULF 756-784 — EAFA

BEORHTRIC 784-800 — EALHMUND

ECGBERT 802-839

AETHELWULF 839-858

AETHELSTAN KING IN KENT 839-851 — AETHELBALD 858-860 — AETHELBERT 860-865 — AETHELRED I 865-871 — ALFRED THE GREAT 871-891

EDWARD THE ELDER 899-924

AETHELSTAN 924-939 — AELFWEARD 924 — EDWIN d 933 — EDMUND I 939-946 — EADRED 946-955

EDWY 955-959 — EADGAR 959-975

EADWARD 975-978 — AETHELRED II 978 - deposed 1013

EADMUND II 1013-1016 — EDWARD 1042-1066 THE CONFESSOR

(FIG. III)

The French term "manoir" was applied,by the clerks collating the Domesday information,to the Saxon holdings which closely resembled their French counterparts.During the tenth and eleventh centuries the manorial system had been evolving in England.The Old English words "heafod botl" (chief dwelling) described the hall and associated buildings at the centre of a Saxon estate.The French were keen to continue the English administration of the economy,to aid collection of taxes and food rents.Initially after 1066 English clerks and writers had continued at their posts in the financial and judicial systems.Record-keeping continued to be done in English until a series of revolts led to ruthless suppression of the English.(Stenton)

Indeed Duke William had hoped for as little disruption as possible.He had hoped to be accepted as King,having been promised the throne by Edward the Confessor who was a cousin.Gilbert Crispin,Archbishop of Westminster 1085-1117,described him as "taking possession of his hereditary kingdom of England".He intended only to replace the Saxon nobility by Normans.He had not bargained for the loathing felt by the Saxons for the invader,nor for the power struggles amongst his own followers.

Since the conversion to Christianity,begun in 595 when the Pope sent Augustine to England,the Anglo-Saxons had developed into an advanced culture.England came to be regarded as a seat of learning by the continental countries.England sent missionaries to convert the Friesians and the Germans. Correspondence flowed between here and the Pope.English books were in great demand. King Alfred (d.899) desired that learning should spread throughout his people and that the Gospels should be available in English.Certainly it was not rare for a layman to read in the tenth century,and a woman's will leaves her "books and such small things",(Whitelock, 1952) perhaps indicating a familiarity with the written word.Priests were expected to be well read and learned in preparation for the questions and discussions that might be put to them by nobles.Later priests in the twelfth and thirteenth centuries often failed in that respect.Despite many battles and skirmishes,the English peoples looked beyond violence to the creation of an ordered society.

In contrast the Normans had nothing to offer but martial arts.They were skilled mounted knights following years of battles for territory in Normandy and northern France,and used to operating as mounted units rather than in single combat.It was this which gave them the edge in the Battle of Hastings.It was their military skills which made them the political masters of Britain.In this it may be said that they were like the Romans.The upper levels of society were now of foreign blood and their contemporary impact was devastating. But now,after 900 years,it is English that is spoken here,the laws can be traced back to those of King Ine and King Alfred,and the Anglo-Saxon culture has now spread to cover large parts of the globe.

Fæder ure þu þe eart on heofonum

Si þin nama gehalgod.

Tobecume þin rice.

Gewurþe ðin willa on eorðan

Swa swa on heofonum.

Urne ge dæghwamlican

Hlaf syle us to-dæg.

And forgyf us ure gyltas,

Swa swa we forgyfað urum gyltendum

And ne gelæd þu us on costnunge,

Ac alys us of yfele.

       Soþlice.

fig iv

Chapter Three

An English Estate

Whatever the type of hamlet at Hungerford it was part of Kintbury
Hundred,an area which today would include Hungerford, Kintbury,
Hamstead and Enborne parishes.A hundred was the financial and
judicial unit and nominally 100 hides.Kintbury Hundred contained
110 hides.The hidage was used to calculate the number of men
required to fight for the King,at one time one man per five
hides,and the amount of feorm due to the King.Round(1895) said
that "assessment bore no ratio to area or value in a vill".Often
a multiple of five hides was applied to a village,this could be
recalculated if a disaster overtook the settlement.The feorm or
firma was rendered initially in produce but towards the late
Saxon period often commuted to cash,between £60 and £80.

Kintbury had begun as a royal estate,but by 1086 the largest
landowner was the Church - Amesbury Abbey.Indeed so strong was
the attachment that until early in the last century the northern
part of Kintbury parish was known as Kintbury- Amesbury despite
the Dissolution in 1547.The abbey's holding is believed to have
been centered at Barton Court.King Edward had two hides at
Kintbury which were probably the village church and market with
houses clustered round and surrounded by the common fields.A
hoard of coins of Kings Edwy and Eadgar (fig.iii) were found in
the village in the early 18th century.

Ramsbury was another royal estate that had become largely a
church holding.There was a large minster at Ramsbury with its own
Bishop from 909.There are known to have been iron works in
Ramsbury in the eighth century and the 1086 survey gives a large
number of ploughs and mills,and a substantial population.(147
households)

Bedwyn was an even larger burh with its own mint(Stenton) and
burgesses.It would have been laid out in "hagas" or hedged plots
that were the same size or larger than the medieval messuage or
tenement.It may have developed as a royal centre from as early as
the sixth century when Cissa,an early west Saxon leader,is
supposed to have been at Chisbury.100 years ago workmen at
Crofton found the skeletal remains of the dead from the Battle of
Bedwyn (675 AD.).Aescwine fought the Mercians and so many died
that no one claimed it as a victory. But Wessex was certainly
more secure and ten years later King Ine began his long rule.He
reputedly had a Saxon palace at Everleigh near Collingbourne.King
Cynewulf granted Little Bedwyn to Earl Bica as "bookland" in
778.The fact that Bedwyn was always a royal estate is indicated
because the Domesday survey says that it never was assessed for
hides as it never paid tax and was still paying "firma unius
noctis". That is,the amount of food-rent required to maintain the
King's court for one night.Bedwyn was an early trading centre.A
law of Edward the Elder (d.924) forbade trading outside a burh or

a "port"(-a trading centre)where his port-reeve could oversee the transactions and collect the tolls due on each.Even the sale of a slave required the payment of a toll, it was fourpence in the time of Edward the Confessor.

Royal estates had initially been very large but grants over the centuries to both lay nobles and churches meant that the king was not always the largest landowner in a district.

The church estates were prominent in the landscape.As is seen from Wulfgar's will it was not unusual for a devout nobleman to bequeathe a large part of his estate to a church, especially if he died childless.The churches were then able to receive all the food-rents for the upkeep of the monastery and employed many dependant peasants.It was not always convenient for the monks or nuns to oversee the work and whole or part estates were leased out to lesser nobles for an initial payment and then a fixed sum due once a year.The work was done by dependant peasants and slaves,the nobleman was not required to do anything beneath his dignity.Leaseholds were generally granted for three lives after which time the land came back to the original owner for re-allocation.Over the years failure to return estates became the source of many disputes.

Surviving Anglo-Saxon poems indicate the pastimes of a nobleman, hunting,hawking,feasting and listening to the harpist,as well as dicing and a game lke chess to pass the evenings. Duties included service in wartime,and attendance at court as well as riding service for the king or hunting fugitives.They were responsible for the good behaviour of their households and would have to represent them in court if the need arose.

The ordinary estates were varied in size.Some were small parts of a formerly large holding that had been divided by the "gavelkind" system of inheritance where all the lord's sons shared equally.The Normans brought inheritance by primo-geniture to England.Some of these small estates were no different in size from peasant holdings,only the owner's rank being different from his neighbour.Other landowners had amassed large acreages by inheritance and careful purchases.But the picture of an average estate had the lord's hall and outbuildings as its central feature,with the church and dependant villagers nearby, surrounded by the lord's land.This can still be seen in many parts of England today.

The bounds of Leverton enclose two square miles or roughly ten hides.The assessment in 1086 was for four and a half hides reduced from six and a half hides in 1066.The assessment could be compared with the modern rateable value, many of the hideages in 1086 indicated a reduced return from the land,not a change in the bounds.

The nobleman had to provide for his dependants.A peasant holding of a house and 30 acres with seven acres already sown,two oxen,one cow and several sheep,with basic tools for the work and equipment for the house may have been a typical outlay(Whitelock).The house was timber,roughly thatched,with a hole in the roof for the smoke to trickle out.If a man's house caught fire and damaged his neighbours he had to pay compensation.In return for the basics,the peasant and his family laboured two or three days each week on the lord's land as well as paying rent and providing produce and livestock at set times of the year.The work load increased at Harvest time and for the autumn ploughing.When he died the property returned to the lord.

In his free time the peasant worked his own land to feed his family,he grew peas and beans in a croft or garden and very occasionally had some meat or fish to enliven a very limited diet.There were no potatoes or tomatoes yet,and no rabbits for the pot until after 1066.Breakfast was bread and ale, lunch — bread and cheese,and supper a bowl of pottage with more bread and cheese,supplemented with fish from the local rivers.The beasts were not often slaughtered for food but kept for milk and wool.Pigs were widely kept as they were most easily fattened up by foraging in the woods.

Class consciousness is not a new phenomenon.The Saxons had a very clear idea of a man's worth.This was not a symbolic but a literal worth.If a man was killed,the "wer-gild" or man-money had to be paid to his kin to prevent an on-going blood feud.A ceorl was worth 200 shillings,a nobleman was worth 1200 shillings.A slave had no wer-gild,he was a chattel worth £1.A nobleman's oath was weightier than that of a peasant,on the other hand a noble would pay a higher fine if convicted of a crime.At the age of 12 a boy was recognised as an adult and admitted as a member of a tithing.Tithing members were responsible for each other's good conduct.King Aethelstan raised the death penalty for stealing from 12 to 15 as he thought it too severe for anyone so young.

The noblewomen were responsible for running the house, weaving,baking and brewing and helping entertain the guests. Children were brought up at home unless destined for the church.If a man died it was thought right that the children remain with their mother,with kinsmen administering their property until they came of age.Women were property owners in their own right,able to bequeath it where they chose,allowed to represent themselves in court and free slaves.In fact they had more freedom than later Norman women.Wulfgar's wife Aeffe is remembered as the owner of Aughton (Aeffeton) Farm at Collingbourne after her husband's death.

Tempus Rex Edwardus — T.R.E.

These initials appear in almost every Domesday Book entry.The survey needed to know the ownership and value of each manor on "the day that King Edward was alive and dead", ie.the day that he died.

The local map (fig v.) appears very similar to the tenth century map, but now much more detail is available.The twentieth century water extraction has substantially lowered the water table.In the eleventh century the local rivers were much fuller and able to power a large number of mills.There were mills at all the local estates,Shalbourn, Bagshot,Standen, Charlton (2),Calcot,Leverton, Eddington and Inkpen.Bedwyn had eight mills,Ramsbury had ten and Kintbury had three.The survey required its commissioners to discover at each manor how many ploughs it could support,how many acres of meadow and woodland,how many slaves, villeins and smallholders it had and the value of the estate at T.R.E. and now.

The survey was conducted by some of the King's nobles,one of whom was Henry de Ferrers who had been rewarded after 1066 by being granted all 22 of the estates that had formerly been managed by Godric the Sheriff,as well as extensive lands in Derbyshire.It was not always clear which manors Godric had managed for the King and which for himself. Each manor was described by Englishmen and Frenchmen with the priest translating,and the scribes noting the details in Latin.Churches were only mentioned occasionally,they were not what the survey was seeking.Ramsbury had a cathedral minster and Kintbury had a minster,that is a church with a graveyard,run by a group of priests.In Bedwyn we see a parish church run by a priest who inherited the position from his father.

There are at least three places that are known to have existed in the tenth century but omitted from the Domesday Book.These are Froxfield,Hidden and Stock.

It is therefore quite feasible for Hungerford to have existed as a hamlet at a river crossing.It could have been included as part of a different manor.Because of the etymology—"ford at a place of hunger",perhaps implying "settlement at a ford at a place where the land is poor",—a past,continuous existence is suggested.Hunger is not a sudden disaster like flood,fire or earthquakes but a condition that takes some time to unfold. Whatever the community that existed at Hungerford,it was not a flourishing farming unit.It was a ford,it was significant as a river crossing,and at a meeting of the ways,from which came its future growth.

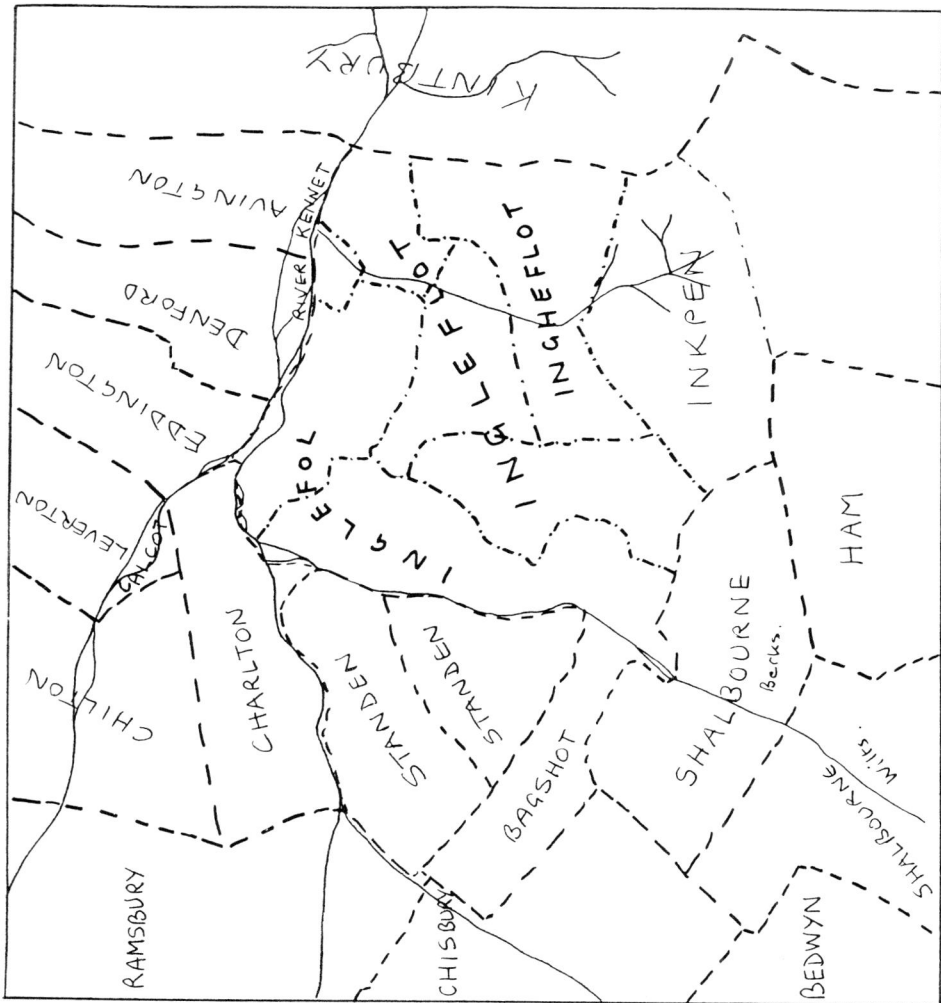

T.R.E. ESTATES
including a possible
division of Inkpen
and Inglewood.

(fig v)   ---- Manors
          ——— Rivers

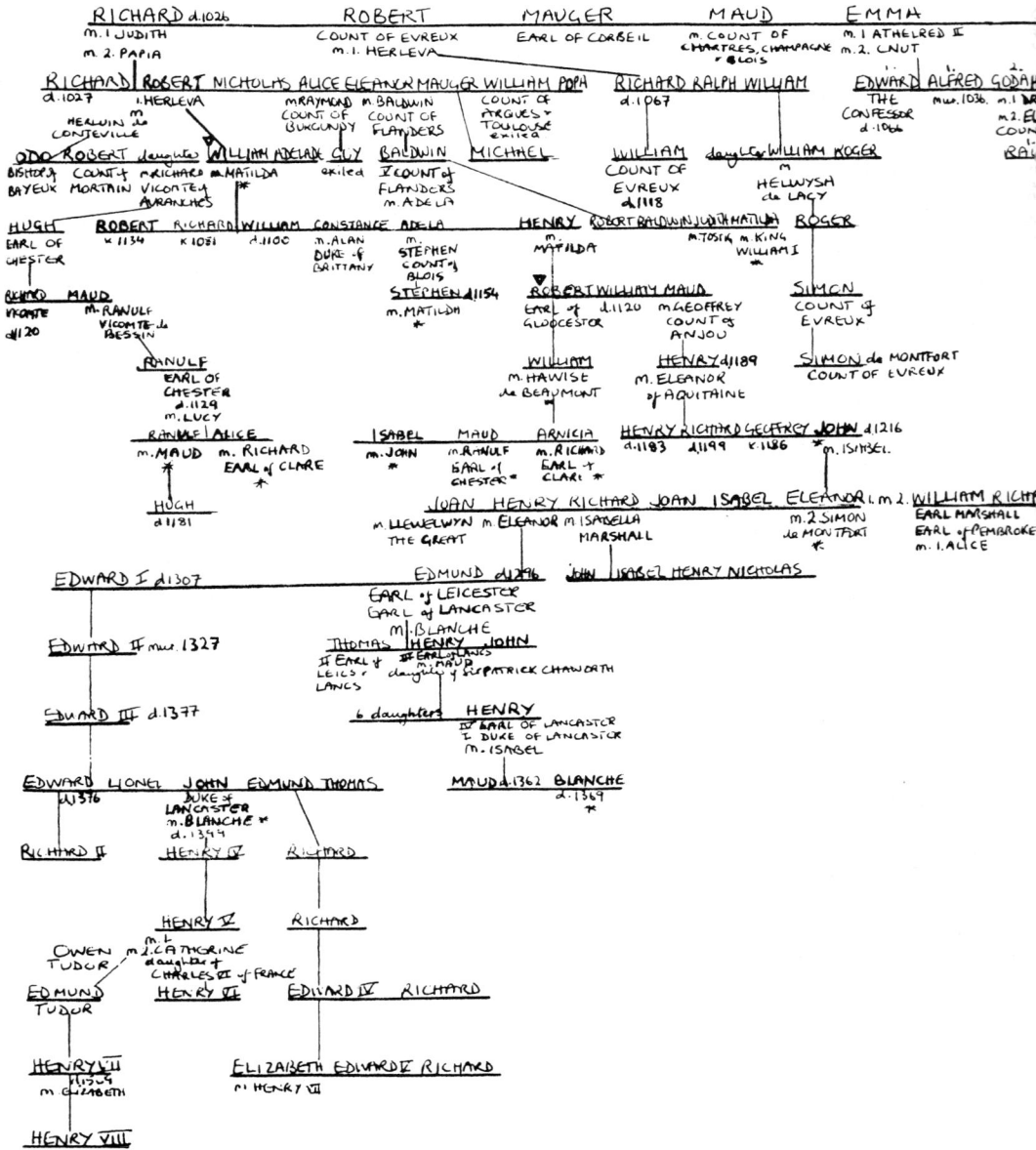

RICHARD d.1026   ROBERT   MAUGER   MAUD   EMMA
m.1 JUDITH   COUNT OF EVREUX   EARL OF CORBEIL   m. COUNT OF   m.1 ATHELRED II
m.2. PAPIA   m.1. HERLEVA   CHARTRES, CHAMPAGNE   m.2. CNUT
            & BLOIS

RICHARD ROBERT NICHOLAS ALICE ELEANOR MAUGER WILLIAM POPA   RICHARD RALPH WILLIAM   EDWARD ALFRED GODAH
d.1027   m.HERLEVA   m.RAYMOND m.BALDWIN COUNT OF   d.1067   THE   mur.1036. m.1 Dt
    HERLUIN de   COUNT OF COUNT OF ARQUES +   CONFESSOR   m.2. EL
    CONTEVILLE   BURGUNDY FLANDERS TOULOUSE   d.1066   COUN
            exiled   RAI

ODO ROBERT daughter WILLIAM ADELAIDE GUY   BALDWIN MICHAEL   WILLIAM   daughter WILLIAM ROGER
BISHOP of COUNT of m.RICHARD m.MATILDA   exiled   II COUNT of   COUNT OF   m
BAYEUX MORTAIN VICOMTE +   *   FLANDERS   EVREUX   HELLWYSH de LACY
    AVRANCHES   m. ADELA   d.1118

HUGH   ROBERT RICHARD WILLIAM CONSTANCE ADELA   HENRY ROBERT BALDWIN JUDITH MATILDA   ROGER
EARL OF   k 1134 k 1081 d.1100 m.ALAN m.   m   m.TOSTI m. KING
CHESTER   DUKE of STEPHEN   MATILDA   WILLIAM I
            BRITTANY COUNT of
                BLOIS

RICHARD MAUD   STEPHEN d.1154   ROBERT WILLIAM MAUD   SIMON
VICOMTE m.RANULF   m.MATILDA   EARL of d.1120 m.GEOFFREY   COUNT of
d.1120 VICOMTE de   *   GLOUCESTER COUNT of   EVREUX
    BESSIN   ANJOU

RANULF   WILLIAM   HENRY d.1189   SIMON de MONTFORT
EARL OF   m.HAWISE   m.ELEANOR   COUNT OF EVREUX
CHESTER   de BEAUMONT   of AQUITAINE
d.1129
m.LUCY

RANULF ALICE   ISABEL MAUD ARNICIA   HENRY RICHARD GEOFFREY JOHN d.1216
m.MAUD m. RICHARD   m.JOHN m.RANULF m. RICHARD   d.1183 d.1199 k.1186 m. ISABEL.
* EARL of CLARE *   * EARL of EARL of
    CHESTER * CLARE *

HUGH   JOAN HENRY RICHARD JOAN ISABEL ELEANOR i.m 2. WILLIAM RICH
d.1181   m LLEWELYN m.ELEANOR m ISABELLA   m.2 SIMON   EARL MARSHALL
    THE GREAT   MARSHALL   de MONTFORT   EARL of PEMBROKE
                m.1.ALICE

EDWARD I d.1307   EDMUND d.1296   JOHN ISABEL HENRY NICHOLAS
        EARL of LEICESTER
        EARL of LANCASTER

EDWARD II mur.1327   m. BLANCHE
        THOMAS HENRY JOHN
        II EARL of III EARL of LANCS
        LEICS + m.MAUD daughter of Sr PATRICK CHAWORTH
        LANCS

EDWARD III d.1377   6 daughters HENRY
            IV EARL OF LANCASTER
            I DUKE OF LANCASTER
            m. ISABEL

EDWARD LIONEL JOHN EDMUND THOMAS   MAUD d.1362 BLANCHE
d.1376   DUKE of   d.1369
    LANCASTER   *
    m.BLANCHE *
    d.1344

RICHARD II   HENRY IV   RICHARD

        HENRY V   RICHARD
        m.1
OWEN   m.2.CATHERINE
TUDOR   daughter of
    CHARLES VI of France
EDMUND   HENRY VI   EDWARD IV RICHARD
TUDOR

HENRY VII   ELIZABETH EDWARD V RICHARD
d.1509   m HENRY VII
m ELIZABETH

HENRY VIII

20

DWISA
FREY
JT of BRITTANY
& RENNES

T GUNHILDA

OGNE
ACE
NT of
OGNE
ARY

LDA

PHEN

a COUSIN — cousin **OSBERN de BOLEBEC** **GEOFFREY** cousin **ALBREDA de la HAYE**
                         LORD of LONGUEVILLE   ? COUNT of BRIONNE   m. HUMPHREY de VIELLES

ROBERT WILLIAM HUGH   **WALTER**   **GILBERT**   **ROGER**
COUNT of   exiled ABBOT of   GIFFARD   COUNT of BRIONNE   LORD OF
EU   LUXEUIL   BEAUMONT
                                                                         m. ADELINE dau of WALERAN
                                                                                 COUNT of MEULAN
WILLIAM   **WALTER** — **ROHAIS** m **RICHARD BALDWIN**   **ROBERT** d.1118
COUNT OF   d.1102   LORD of   COUNT OF MEULAN
EU   CLARE   m. ISABEL
1096 - forfeited
lands to Earls Marshall   **GILBERT**   b.1104
                                               EARL of CLARE   **WALERAN ROBERT d.1163 HUGH**
                                               d.1116   COUNT of EARL OF
                                                               MEULAN   LEICESTER
                                                               m. AGNES m. AMICIA

GILBERT MARSHALL   **GILBERT RICHARD**   **ROBERT ISABEL HAWISE**
                           EARL of CLARE EARL of CLARE   EARL OF m SIMON m. WILLIAM
                           EARL of PEMBROKE EARL of HERTFORD LEICESTER EARL of FITZ ROBERT
                                           m. ALICE   m. PARNEL HUNTINGDON EATE & GLOS
JOHN   **RICHARD** **GILBERT ROGER**   **AMICIA ROBERT**   MARGARET
MARSHALL of ENGLAND   de CLARE   EARL of   m. SIMON de d.1205 m. SAHER de
m. SYBIL   EARL of PLANTAGENET HERTFORD   MONTFORT EARL of   QUINCY
                           m. EVA daughter of   LEICESTER
                           KING DERMOT   **RICHARD**   **SIMON** d.1218 **ROGER**
2.   m. ARNICIA   EARL of LEICESTER
WILLIAM   m   **ISABEL**   *   m. ALICE
EARL MARSHALL
EARL of PEMBROKE   **RICHARD**   **AMAURI** **SIMON** K.1265 **MARGARET**
d.1219.   m. ARNICIA   EARL of LEICESTER m. WILLIAM
                                          *   m. ELEANOR   de FERRERS
RT WALTER ANSELM MAUD SYBILLA EVA JOHANNA ISABELLA 2 m i **GILBERT**   EARL of DERBY
         m.HUGH m.WILLIAM   *   m. RICHARD EARL of CLARE & HERTFORD
         EARL of de FERRERS   EARL of GLOUCESTER   **ROBERT**
         NORFOLK EARL of   d.1230   lost estates
         EARL   DERBY   **RICHARD**   **HENRY SIMON GUY ELEANOR AUMERLE** to Crown
         MARSHALL   EARL of HERTFORD K.1265   m. LLEWELLYN
                                          & GLOUCESTER   THE LAST
                                          d.1262

                                          GILBERT
                                          EARL of HERTFORD
                                          & GLOUCESTER
                                          d.1295

DESCENDANTS OF ROLF
    1st DUKE OF NORMANDY

✴ MARRIED TO DISTANT COUSIN
▽ ILLEGITIMATE

Local landowners included Counts Evreux, Eu & Meulan
and de Ferrers and de Chuworth. All these lands
were brought together under John O'Gaunt.

(fig vi)

Chapter Four

The Norman Conquest

Of all the knights who came to England with William,at the most only 40 are proved by contemporary record to have been at the Battle of Hastings.One of these was Robert Beaumont, Count of Meulan,who became the owner of Eddington and later Hungerford. Robert's son became Earl of Leicester and inherited his father's English lands and honours.But there is no record of their links with Hungerford in the Domesday Book.

The Domesday Book is a colossal monument to Anglo-Norman cooperation,and the earliest record of its kind in the world. From it we have a picture of the structure of society in the eleventh century.It is very frustrating that there is no record of Hungerford's existence.Until now it has been assumed that Hungerford did not exist prior to 1086 but grew up within one generation of that time.The earlier chapters have tried to show that this may not have been the case.

For the first few generations after the Conquest the Normans regarded their English lands as a secondary interest.Their eldest sons inherited their lands in Normandy,even in the case of King William and his eldest son Duke Robert.The second son became the lord of the English possessions.And a number of the knights returned to Normandy having refused lands in England,seeing a better future on the continent.

Robert Beaumont was a distant cousin of King William.(fig.vi) His father Roger was Lord of Beaumont,now Beaumont-le-Roger in Eure. Through his mother he inherited the title Count of Meulan.This maternal inheritance frequently happened to early titles as nobles' sons often perished in battles and jousts, if they survived infancy.Robert married twice,firstly to Emma de Breteuil and secondly,to Isabel -grandaughter of the King of France,in 1096/7;Waleran,the elder of his twin sons born in 1104,became Count of Meulan and Robert became the English lord.

It is through Count Robert that the earliest mention of Hungerford is discovered.Some time before his death in 1118 he granted to the church of the Holy Trinity in Beaumont the manor of Eddington by Hungerford.The partial ruins of the Priory in Beaumont are still visible today.

The Normans were devout,founding very many churches,priories, abbeys and nunneries in both Normandy and England.This devotion did not seem to have any effect on their warlike life-styles. However they did deplore the slavery they found in Britain and freed many of the slaves on their manors.It was often the case that towards the end of his life the Norman lord became genuinely devout and spent his remaining years in an abbey.

Roger and Count Robert founded the Abbey at Preaux where Roger retired in 1090 until his death in 1099.Hastings was the first battle for Robert,and he acquitted himself well.Summers says that he was rewarded with 90 baronies,but he does not give details,Round says lands in Warwickshire.Ivo de Grandmesnil,Lord of Leicester,ran away during the battle for Antioch.To expiate his guilt,he went on another crusade to Jerusalem with his wife.He had to mortgage his estates to Robert Beaumont to raise the money.Both Ivo and his wife died on the journey in 1102,and Robert kept the estates, including the town of Leicester, disinheriting young Ivo II.

Earl Robert founded the Abbey of St.Mary at Leicester,the monastery at Nuneaton, the priory at Lusfield and the hospital at Brackley as well as many smaller houses.One of these was recorded in a grant of 25 librates of land in Kintbury and the soke of Hungerford for making a convent of nuns of the order of Fontevrault (1147)(V.C.H.Berks.).This gift was later transferred to the Priory of Nuneaton.The land became known as Kintbury-Eaton,and is situated around Kintbury Holt.Robert granted some land to Bec,and also granted tithes from his own property to Bec.In the early twelfth century Bec had acquired the tithes of Inglefol (Summers).Can Inglefol be linked to Robert this way?

The term "soke" refers to the manorial jurisdiction.Stenton says that by 1066 an unusual type of estate had arisen with sokemen,singly or in groups,scattered in many villages but still owing rents and customary services to a central manor.This was seen more often in the Danelaw but still occurred in other parts of the country.It might reasonably be assumed that by 1147 Hungerford was seen as having jurisdiction over a defined area of land and named individuals.

The descent of manors is sometimes confusing as there were many power struggles after the conquest.Some former favourites or relatives of the King were tried for treason, and forfeited their lands.Amongst these was William of Eu,a cousin of King William,who was accused of treason in 1096 by Geoffrey Bainard.He lost in trial by combat,was blinded and mutilated by order of the King and forfeited his lands.The new owners of Charlton were the Marshalls who managed it until the mid-thirteenth century.Another local landowner who was accused at that time was Arnulf de Hesdin.He owned North Standen and part of Buttermere. Despite the entreaties of the King,assured of his innocence,he left the country for Jerusalem and never returned.The ownership of some of his property seems to have descended through his daughter Maud to her husband's family —the de Chaworths,and from them eventually to the Duchy of Lancaster.

The term ownership is used,but it must be remembered that the lands were held by the King's goodwill and were liable to forfeit and could be regranted elsewhere.On the accession of a new king or new heir to a property the grant could be re-affirmed.

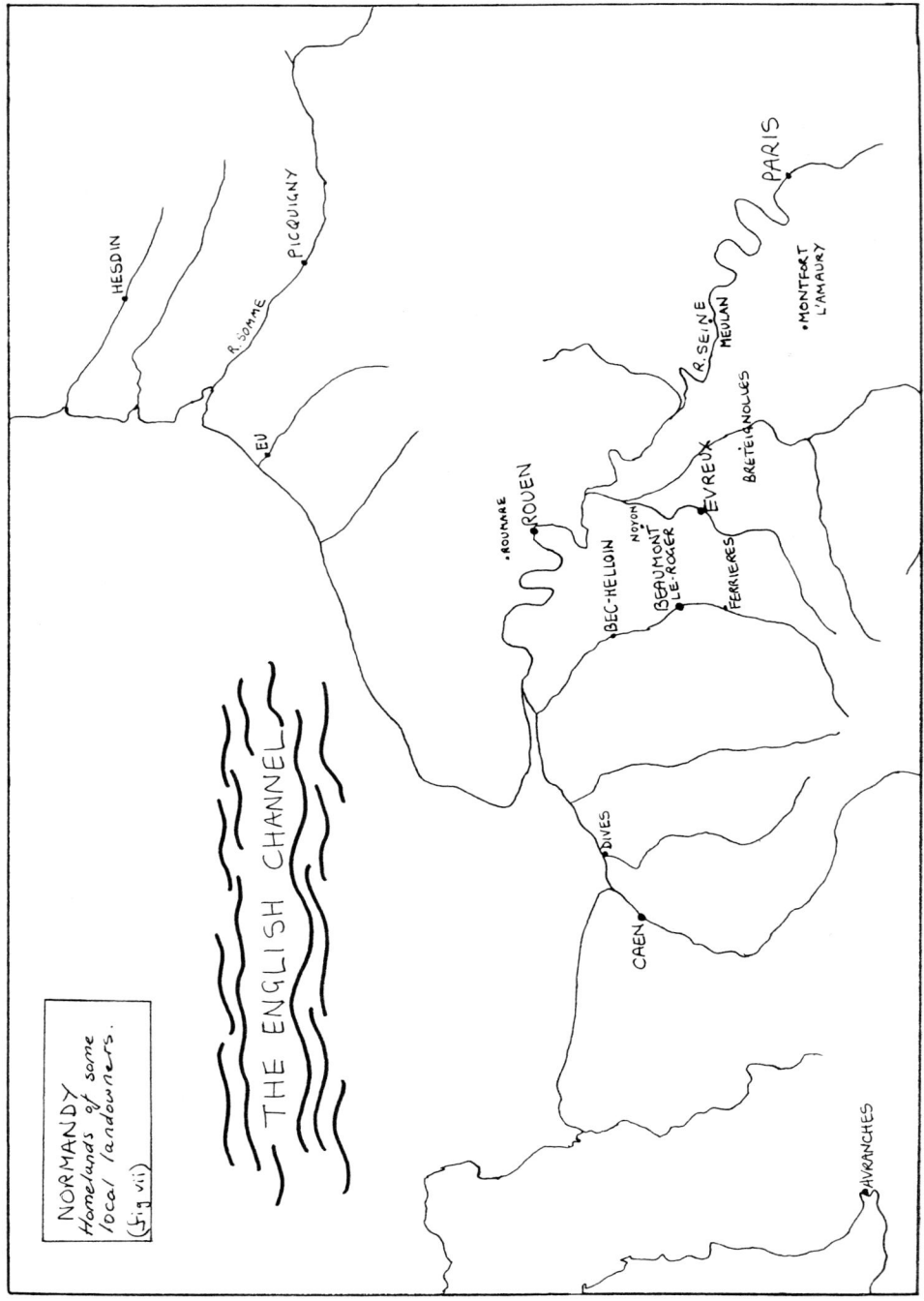

NORMANDY
Homelands of some
local landowners.
(Fig vii)

THE ENGLISH CHANNEL

HESDIN

PICQUIGNY

R. SOMME

EU

ROUMARE

ROUEN

BEC-HELLOIN

NOYON

BEAUMONT
LE-ROGER

FERRIERES

EVREUX

BRÉTEUANOLLÉS

MEULAN

R. SEINE

MONTFORT
L'AMAURY

PARIS

DIVES

CAEN

AVRANCHES

24

Similarly the numerous grants to religious houses were re-affirmed by lords on their inheritance.A charter of Earl Robert renewing his family's grant to the church of St. Leger at Preaux has survived (1121-1135).He makes the grant as did his father and grandfather before him,making reference to the consent obtained from King William I and King William II to do so.This charter is remarkable for the first recorded reference to William I as "the conqueror". It also refers to "his exchequer" into which past rents have been paid.The great Earls modelled their households on that of the king. Robert was the first Earl of Leicester,the title having been created after his inheritance following his father's seizure of that county.In 1140 King Stephen created him Earl of Hereford.He became Chief Justiciar in 1155/56 and then Regent during the absence of Henry II in France in 1158-63.

Leicester was a borough in the Danelaw that had an Anglo-Saxon mint,a cathedral minster and a minster church before the conquest. Robert, Count of Meulan was a powerful and respected baron,one of about a dozen confidantes and counsellors of the King who had rewarded him with extensive lands and honours.He understood the mechanics of borough administration and the profits to be made.A charter of Henry I requires that the Sheriff of Oxford give Earl Robert's men the benefit of the same customs that he gave them in the time of his father the Count.People had moved to the towns for freedom and profits,and this profit was passed on to the founder (ecclesiastical or lay) of the borough.The notion of a new borough at Hungerford would have appealed as a better use of poor land. More will be said about the nature of boroughs in a later chapter.

Two other local landowners have already been mentioned. William d'Eu and Arnulf de Hesdin,to their number must be added the Count d'Evreux,Henry de Ferrers,Robert FitzGerald de Roumare and William son of Ansculf,Vidame de Picquigny. Counts Eu and Evreux can be found on the family tree (fig.vi).The map(fig.vii) shows where their homes were.As has been stated,many saw their Norman lands as more important, and frequently sent profits from English lands to endow Norman religious foundations.Whole villages were granted to Bec Abbey.This meant that the tithes,rents and services were commuted to cash to benefit the alien church or that the benefits went to an English cell or offshoot of that alien foundation.

The Benedictine Abbey of Notre-Dame at Bec-Helloin was founded by Herluin in 1034.Lanfranc,Archbishop of Canterbury from 1070-1089, trained there.It still exists today having been reconsecrated in 1948 by the Benedictine Order.Ogbourne was granted to Bec in 1149 and became the richest Benedictine cell in England.The Priory of St.John the Baptist at Hungerford was also a Benedictine cell.

Chapter Five

The Growth of the Church

In Saxon times the church had grown steadily with grants and endowments from king and nobles alike.But from the time of the conquest the church saw an enormous surge in growth,and parish boundaries became permanent as each religious house sought to maintain its area of influence.The period from 1070 —1170 saw the foundation of a church in almost every English parish as well as numerous monasteries.Some began as private chapels belonging to the landowner for his personal use,some of these were converted to parish use,others fell into decay.

The sites of churches have provoked much discussion.Pope Gregory's first instruction to Augustine in June 595 had been to destroy all pagan sites and to convert the heathen.He later changed his mind.The English paganism was similar to that found in other parts of the world — a superstitious acknowledgement of the power and rhythmic changes of the seasons.The Pope's new instruction was to cleanse the sites of their pagan features and then to encourage people to come to the same place to worship God.Some churches therefore have been built on ancient sites, often near springs,sacred groves or trees,and standing stones.Of course the first churches were wooden and traces do not survive easily,but from the time of Alfred some churches were built in stone.These stone churches also provide much food for thought as Roman building stones have been found in present-day church walls.It has been mooted that in some places there may have been continuity of worship from Romano-British Christianity,though this is felt to have been unlikely.Some other churches began as monastic cells on rough terrain or at secluded or isolated sites.

Unfortunately none of these criteria can be seen to apply to the site of Hungerford's church.The building itself is less than 200 years old,replacing one that was believed to have had some 14th century features,no references to springs or groves have been found.It is situated some way from the High Street and the town centre,was it possibly a secluded site?.Having said that,it can be seen from the map(fig.viii)that not all churches are in the centres of their villages,not many are the focal point of even the oldest parts of the villages.

Where a church is situated near a manor house (or manor farm,which often indicates an earlier presence of a manor house)it was possibly on the site of an earlier private Norman chapel.Where the church is in the village it could be on the site of an earlier Saxon church.Where the church is some way removed from the village it is possible that it is on the site of an earlier and now disappeared village or private house.From the 12th century villages were not static,and by the 14th there were

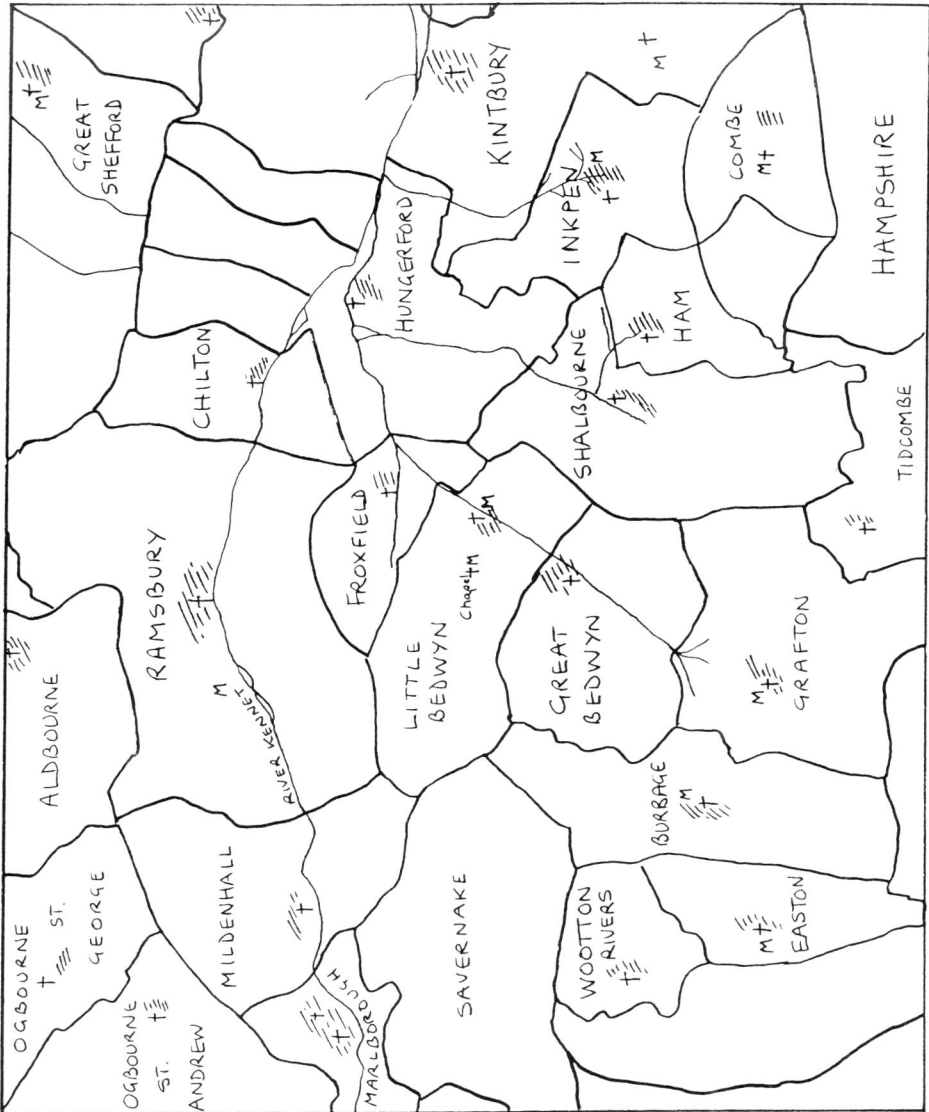

CHURCHES
(fig. viii)

KEY
† PARISH CHURCH
M MANOR FM/HO.
▨ AREA OF VILLAGE

GREAT SHEFFORD

KINTBURY

COMBE

HAMPSHIRE

INKPEN

HAM

HUNGERFORD

CHILTON

SHALBOURNE

TIDCOMBE

RAMSBURY

FROXFIELD

LITTLE BEDWYN

GREAT BEDWYN

GRAFTON

ALDBOURNE

RIVER KENNET

SAVERNAKE

BURBAGE

EASTON

OGBOURNE ST. GEORGE

OGBOURNE ST. ANDREW

MILDENHALL

MARLBOROUGH

WOOTTON RIVERS

many solitary churches as monuments to village movement.Because ecclesiastical records did not begin until the thirteenth century,the foundation of the majority of parish churches is not recorded.In Hungerford's case,partly because it did not appear in the Domesday Book,it is known that the High Street formed the basis of a new town founded by the Normans.St.Lawrence's church,if it existed on its present site, was obviously considered near enough to the centre to be convenient,or the Normans would have moved it.A Lincolnshire village church was moved in 1180 when a lord gave land for a new site and the bodies were dug up for reburial (Morris,R 1989).Or possibly the townspeople worshipped in the nave of the Priory of St.John at the north end of the town.Hungerford's church could have been in a small hamlet in the Croft,though it is difficult to see why it was not in Domesday Book if the hamlet was big enough to warrant a church.Unless the hamlet had another name.

Another possibilty is raised by the coincidental existence in Hungerford of the Sisters of St.Lawrence who ran a hospital for lepers.Did they have their foundation on the site of the present church of St.Lawrence,and when their house failed the chapel became a parish church?The Sisters are mentioned in the bounds of a perambulation of Savernake Forest in 1232.A recitation of the 1300 bounds is considered by Adams(1910) to have touched Hungerford on the south west and may support that theory.

At some stage assumptions have to be made.The evidence is circumstantial,but it could be concluded that a small early settlement called Hungerford existed in what is now Bridge Street and The Forge.This would have been a river crossing with possibly a long history dating from the sixth century. This was not a successful farming community,but a tiny hamlet on the junction of routes to Ramsbury,Bedwyn, Kintbury and very much further afield.

There may have been a separate manor centered on the site of a church that had been erected by the lord.Churches are often found on the edge of the manorial enclosure (fig.viii).On that basis,either the Old Parsonage or "Tumblings" might be a possible site for a manor house.The manor could possibly have been the Inglefol of the Domesday Book that had been two manors in the time of King Edward.The other half of that three-hide manor could have been one of the other tithings that came to form Hungerford.

Through Robert Beaumont the land south of the river became united,giving the opportunity to found a totally new town rather in the manor of Bracknell,Stevenage,Basildon etc.,on a greenfield site.

Chapter Six

The Borough of Hungerford

The borough of Hungerford had definitely been created by 1173.This is proved by the townsmen having the right of "firma burgi" during the disgrace of the 2nd Earl of Leicester (1173-1177) (VCHBerks).As already stated "firma" was the Latin for "feorm",an Old English word meaning food-rent payable to the King,or to the lay or ecclesiastical lord."Burgi",the genitive case of burh or borough,means "of the borough". Hence the conclusion that Hungerford was a borough.

In the early twelfth century Robert Beaumont,Count of Meulan, owned Eddington and described it in a grant to Beaumont church as "Eddevetona by Hungreford"(1101-1118,VCH Berks.)The question here must be-"was Hungerford a borough by the time of that grant"?At the moment it is unanswerable. If Hungerford had been a Saxon or very early Norman borough it would have appeared in the Domesday Book,which was not the case. Therefore the foundation of the Borough of Hungerford can be dated somewhere between 1086 and 1173.

The 1142 grant by Waleran Beaumont,Count of Meulan,giving Beaumont Church to the Abbey of Bec fuelled a dispute between St.Frideswides Priory at Oxford and Bec.It was resolved by the Pope in 1147 by St.Frideswides having Eddington (granted to Beaumont in 1101-1118) and Hidden,but giving a third of the villein's tithe to Hungerford Church.The settlement refers to - "Hungerford,in whose parish Eddington is".In common with other parts of the country the parish bounds had become firmly fixed by the middle of the twelfth century,and it would appear that Hungerford Church was the parish church.This "Hungerford Church" is thought to refer to the Benedictine Priory of St.John the Baptist,an offshoot of Bec,rather than St. Lawrence's Church.Stenton says that a Norman lord could set aside 2/3 of his tithes to benefit any church,notwithstanding the prior claims of an established minster.There is a suggestion implicit in the settlement that Waleran's grant had somehow upset this previous 1/3 and 2/3 split,that Hungerford's loyalty to Bec was firmly established and that Hungerford Priory existed at least as early as 1142.Was the borough formed at the same time as the Priory?

No charters have survived for the foundation of the Priory and the Borough,but they must certainly have existed as a statement of the rights and duties of the inhabitants,and to ensure both their profits and those of the lord.

As seen in chapter four Robert Beaumont,Count of Meulan did not acquire Leicester until 1102.Right up until his death in 1118 he was being asked to return the estates to the Grandmesnil heir.The

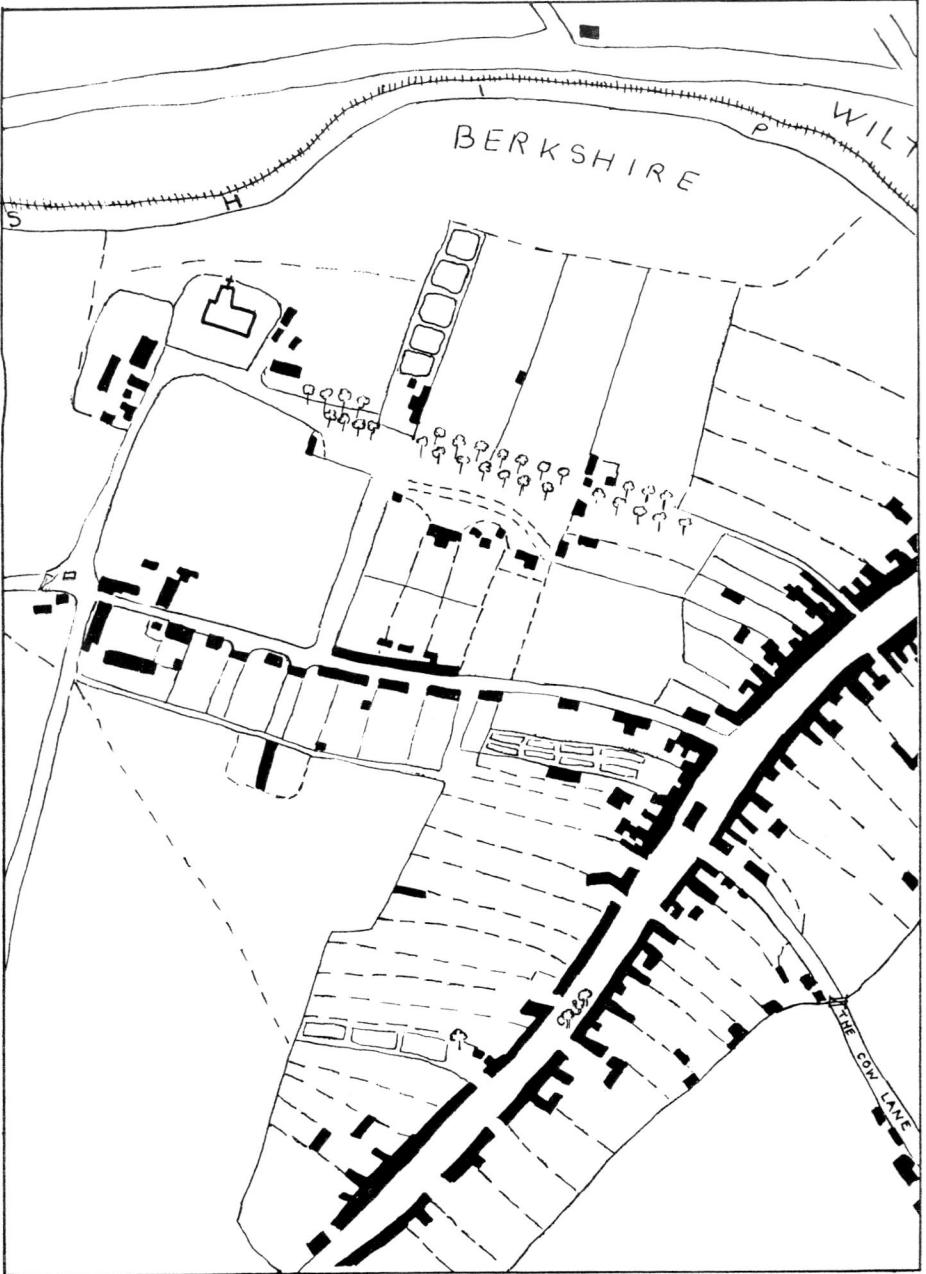

BERKSHIRE

WILT

THE COW LANE

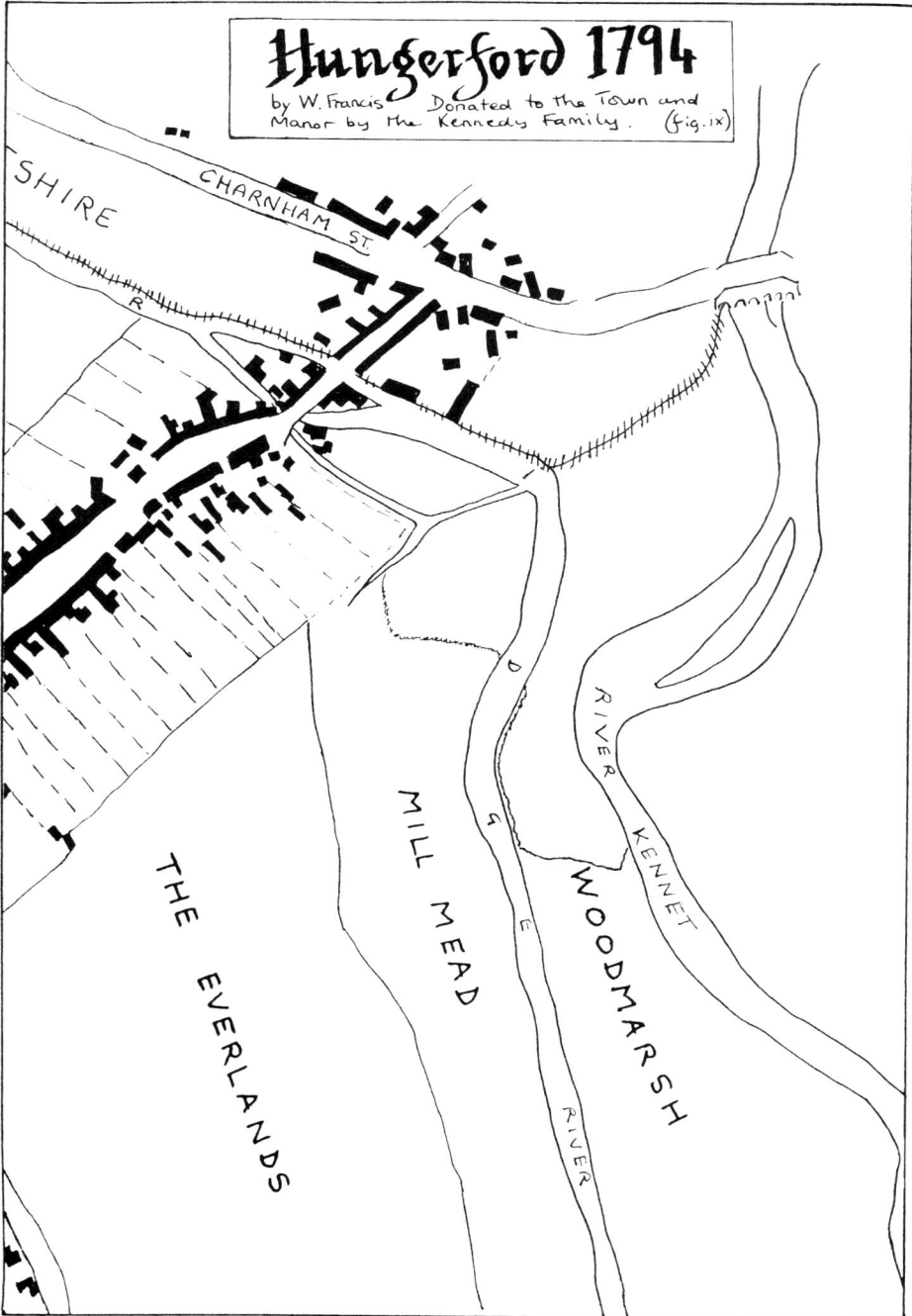

Hungerford 1794

by W. Francis Donated to the Town and Manor by the Kennedy Family. (fig. ix)

CHARNHAM ST.

SHIRE

R

MILL MEAD

THE EVERLANDS

WOODMARSH

RIVER KENNET

RIVER

lands in Warwickshire that he received from William I as a reward for his loyal service are not named.But Eddington was still in the King's hands at the time of the Domesday Survey.It must have been as a reward from William II that Robert Beaumont received Eddington,possibly for service in France in 1096-7 against Duke Robert.He remarried at this time,possibly arranged by the King for strategic ends.Robert may have gained Inglefol during this period,as Robert Fitz-Gerald of Roumare left no direct heir.Summers says that Bec had tithes from Inglefol,was this possibly as a gift from the Beaumonts? The foundation of the Borough of Hungerford might then be dated between c.1096 and c.1142.

In the 1170's the Earl of Leicester had a Court at Hidden, held at Martinmas.The burgesses from Hungerford attended this court as its jurisdiction was older than that of the borough (Hidden,N).But they were all Earl Robert's men.The traders of Hungerford did not want the vill of Eddington to benefit from the bed and board involved in hosting a court,though naturally Eddington would benefit from any fines imposed during court proceedings.Here again is evidence of Hungerford's identity as a trading centre not a farm.

A successful market town was much more profitable to its lord than farm tenants.Many abbots,bishops and large landowners gained the vital royal charter and laid out their new towns. Occupants were attracted by the special privileges they would receive.One was the right,only granted by the king or lord,to hold a fair or market.If the town were laid out along an existing road rather than at a junction,then the need for a street frontage made the town whatever length was required to give each burgess an outlet.At one end of the street there would generally be a market place or the church,or the street might be broadened in the middle for the market place.The desire for a good trading place meant that the side streets were never developed to the same extent and the population overall was not large.From 1086 onwards the rights and duties of the citizens became clearer.The status of the burghers was the central point.They held free tenure and were the sole practitioners of their trade or craft within the borough.In this can be seen the essence of the medieval gilds.

The long,narrow burgage plots affected the design of the houses put upon them.Essentially they were the rural hall or long house with a narrow access passage at one side.At the rear a courtyard opened out slightly to provide light,and the necessary smaller outbuildings stretched back in a line.This is instantly identifiable with many of Hungerford's High Street properties.The total shape of the narrow plot might be affected by a stream or steep slope,or a previously erected church or monastery(Platt).It is unlikely that the previous open field furrows affected the shape as they were entirely built over at the lord's directive.The suggestion that early medieval farmers ploughed an S shaped furrow is also suspect.Bennett says that field strips of up to an acre ran parallel for the whole length of the furlong and were divided by raised balks of unploughed land.The "headlands",or unploughed strips for access,were at right angles to these.The High St. follows the shallowest gradient up the hill and consequently bends.Church St. is virtually level as it curves along the contour on the side of the steep slope of Prospect Rd.It was probably these existing streets that caused the burgage plots to bend as they do.Notice how the plots became shorter towards the south.The whole Norman town was tucked neatly into a fold of land along the road to Salisbury.

A typical burgage plot might be 60 feet wide and 200 feet deep.Within decades these lots were divided into two or three subdivisions as traders found it more profitable to lease or sell part of their land.The important thing was to keep a shop-front from which to trade.Hungerford's design was purely as a trading centre,it was undefended and indefensible.The Kennedy map(fig ix) probably shows the town virtually unchanged from very soon after its foundation.It is believed that part of the fabric of Roxton's shop dates from the fourteenth century.Possibly other High Street and Bridge Street shops and houses have also incorporated earlier Norman buildings. The oldest artefact known in Hungerford is the sadly mutilated effigy of Sir Robert de Hungerford that dates from soon after his death in 1352.It can be found in the church with a tablet bearing a Norman-French inscription.The Kennedy map is the earliest surviving detailed plan of the town.It is interesting to see the town before the railway and canal, subsequent development to the north was prevented by them.

The foundation of burhs created a new class of person who fell outside the traditional feudal system.The burghers or burgesses were freemen,owning their property,owing no service only rents to the lord who founded the burh.The property could be sold,leased or bequeathed to relatives as long as proof of ownership existed.A runaway villein who took shelter in a burh could,if he stayed there for a year and a day,be given the freedom of the burh.He could not then be taken back to his erstwhile lord.The towns attracted many traders who kept a pig and some hens in the long narrow garden and grew vegetables and some fruit.Sheep and cattle could be grazed on the common.But they relied heavily on the surrounding agricultural community for provisions.This gave a boost to the small farmers in the surrounding area.It is interesting to note that Hungerford is approximately 10 miles from Newbury and Marlborough,and a little more from Wantage and Andover. This distance represented the furthest journey required for a day trip to markets or fairs.The community in Hungerford would be self-contained,making as many of its requisites as possible. Ramsbury,Kintbury,Bedwyn and Lambourn,all early Saxon centres were less important to the Normans.Marlborough,Hungerford and Newbury were all vital to the communications network.Both Marlborough and Newbury had castles,though there has never been any suggestion of a castle at Hungerford.

Chapter Seven

Town and Country

The Beaumonts held the Earldom of Leicester until the death of
Robert,the third Earl,in 1205.Under their management the market
town must have prospered.It seems likely that what is described
as the Town Tithing on the Enclosure map of 1819 formed the basis
of the town.This included the Port Down where the townspeople
held shared grazing,the cattle were driven up Cow lane,now Park
Street.The ditch and bank which enclosed the old Port Down can
still be traced today.Also included were the Everlong Field,
which stretched all the way to Denford,and Woodmarsh which lay
between the Dun and the Kennet. Early medieval farming practices
relied on the manuring of arable fields by flocks of sheep
recently grazed on wet fresh grass.Two sheep bridges led from the
Woodmarsh up to the Everlong,where the field divisions can still
be seen,now bisected by the railway.The 1794 mapmaker W.Francis
must have been told by local people that the smaller of the two
rivers was called the Sheep Bridge river,as he has labelled it
the "ship ridge river".On the Enclosure map it is simply called
the Old River."Theofait" or thief island,first mentioned in
1200,is thought to have been the island in the Kennet,perhaps an
early gaol.

It is likely that this Town Tithing was the land of one of the
two manors which formed the 1086 Inglefol.Again looking at the
Enclosure Award it might be possible that the other of those two
manors is what came to be known as the Sandon Fee Tithing.This
included all the land between the Shalbourn stream and Sanham
Green,south of the town towards Prosperous. This coincidence of
the name "san"—OE for sand,and "don" meaning downland and the
hamlet at Sanham Green would support this theory.The management
of this manor was leased out to Gilbert de Breteignolles as a
knight's fee.This meant he had to provide the service of one
knight for his lord the Earl of Leicester.The Earl had to provide
a certain number of knights for the king.Many great landowners
created more fees than were required to create extra
income.Knight's fees could be sub-let and sub-divided but payment
for the fractions had to be commuted to cash.The cash paid for
the maintenance of a standing body of armed troops.

In this way the Earl,like many others,added to his wealth.He had
an annual income from the town of Hungerford,income from his
court at Eddington and Hidden,and one knight provided for his
troop by Sandon.A much more profitable arrangement than the "poor
land at the ford".Between them the Earl's bailiff and the town's
port-reeve managed everything.In this instance for some time at
least,the profits were split between the Abbey of Bec for its
local cells at Ogbourn or Hungerford,or the Priory of
St.Frideswides who benefitted from Eddington.After his death in
1205 Robert was succeeded by his nephews.The Beaumont inheritance
was divided between the de Montfort and the de Quincy heirs.The
de Montfort half included the Earldom of Leicester, the title

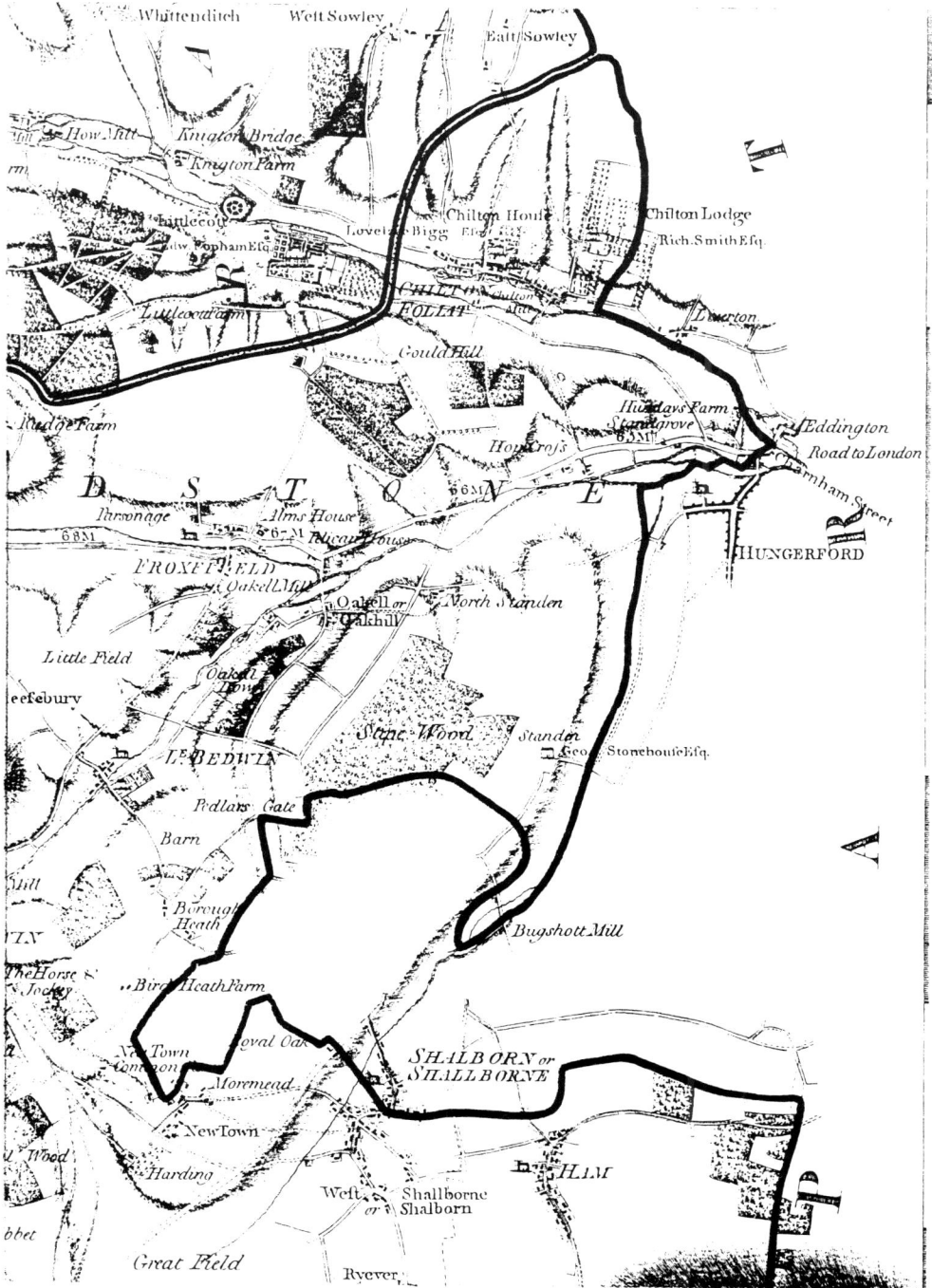

ANDREWS & DURY MAP 1773

Whittenditch   Weft Sowley   Eaft Sowley

How Mill   Knighton Bridge
Knighton Farm

Littlecot   Chilton Houfe   Chilton Lodge
Ldw. Popham Efq.   Lovel Bigg Efq.   Rich. Smith Efq.

CHILTON
FOLIAT   Eſſrerton

Littlecot Farm

Gould Hill

Husbays Farm   Eddington
Standgrove   Road to London
65 M.

Hop Crofs   Cernham Street

D   S   T   O   N   E

Parsonage   Alms House   66 M.   HUNGERFORD

68 M.   Alican Houfe

FROXFIELD
Oakell Mill

Little Field   Oakell or   North Standen
Oakhill

eefebury

Oakell
Town   Stne Wood   Standen
Geo. Stonehoufe Efq.

L. BEDWIN

Pedlars Gate

Barn

Borough
Heath   Bugshott Mill

Mill

The Horse &   Birch Heath Farm
Jockey

New Town   Royal Oak   SHALBORN or
Common   SHALLBORNE

Moremead

New Town   H.L.M.

Harding

Weft   Shallborne
or   Shalborn

Wood

Great Field   Ryever

bbet

35

Steward of England,and half the lands.These included about sixty knights fees.The total revenues of this half were quite small,only £256 in 1207. Robert's nephew Simon had forfeited his inheritance in 1207 and it was managed by the Crown until 1218 when Simon died, and then by the Earl of Chester until 1230.At that time Simon's son,also Simon,came to England.He had been in France on the family estates that were run by his elder brother Amaury.Simon successfully persuaded Henry III not only that he was entitled to the earldom,but that he was a suitable husband for Henry's daughter Eleanor.She had been widowed at the age of 16 when William Marshall,Earl of Pembroke died, and eventually brought Simon her share of the Marshall inheritance.As a widow she was supposed to receive one third. It took her many years to prove her claim as William had been succeeded in turn by his four brothers.The king gave the earl Kenilworth and Odiham castles and these together with Dover were the main homes of the couple.A great landowner would move his household around the country visiting his different properties to ensure that they were well run.Earl Simon complained that when he took over his lands they had been badly mismanaged by the royal bailiffs (Labarge),and that some of the woods and forests had been destroyed.Presumably his "wood of Bauteley"that he received licence to enclose in 1246 (VCHBerks) had survived this blight as he was able to create Hungerford park,though he probably did not visit it very often.This licence was granted despite the land being within the bounds of Savernake Forest.

Various perambulations of Savernake Forest in the thirteenth century are believed to have included Hungerford in the region where Forest Law applied.Penalties for poaching game in such an area were severe.This did not mean however that the whole region was heavily forested.The actual forest was composed of a number of bailiwicks,— the West Bailiwick comprising the Great Park and centre of Pewsey Vale,the East that is Savernake itself with almost the same bounds as today,a wood at Southgrove,and Bedwyn Bailiwick which included Stype Wood and ran south to include Harding Farm; Southstones and Hippingscombe.The 1300 bounds are recited in both Adams and the WAM.It seems that Berkshire Forest law applied as far west as the Inge stream.This would have been overseen by Walter Fitz Othere who held half a hide in Kintbury as Keeper of the Forest. Walter was Castellan of Windsor and held land in Berkshire, Buckinghamshire, Surrey, Hampshire and Middlesex.According to Lysons,the Vale of Kennet was disforested by charter in 1226.

Did this mean that Forest Law ceased to apply except in wooded areas?Did this encourage more settlement?A family needed between 36 and 40 bushels of grain which required at least ten acres(Bennett).An average family holding of 30 acres for a dependant peasant would be made up of many strips to be found in many separate fields around the village.This would give a reasonable standard of living in good weather. But many men held much less land than this and had to find other ways to supplement their income,perhaps by helping at the manor or by taking up a trade. And misfortune could befall anyone. In 1275 eight free men

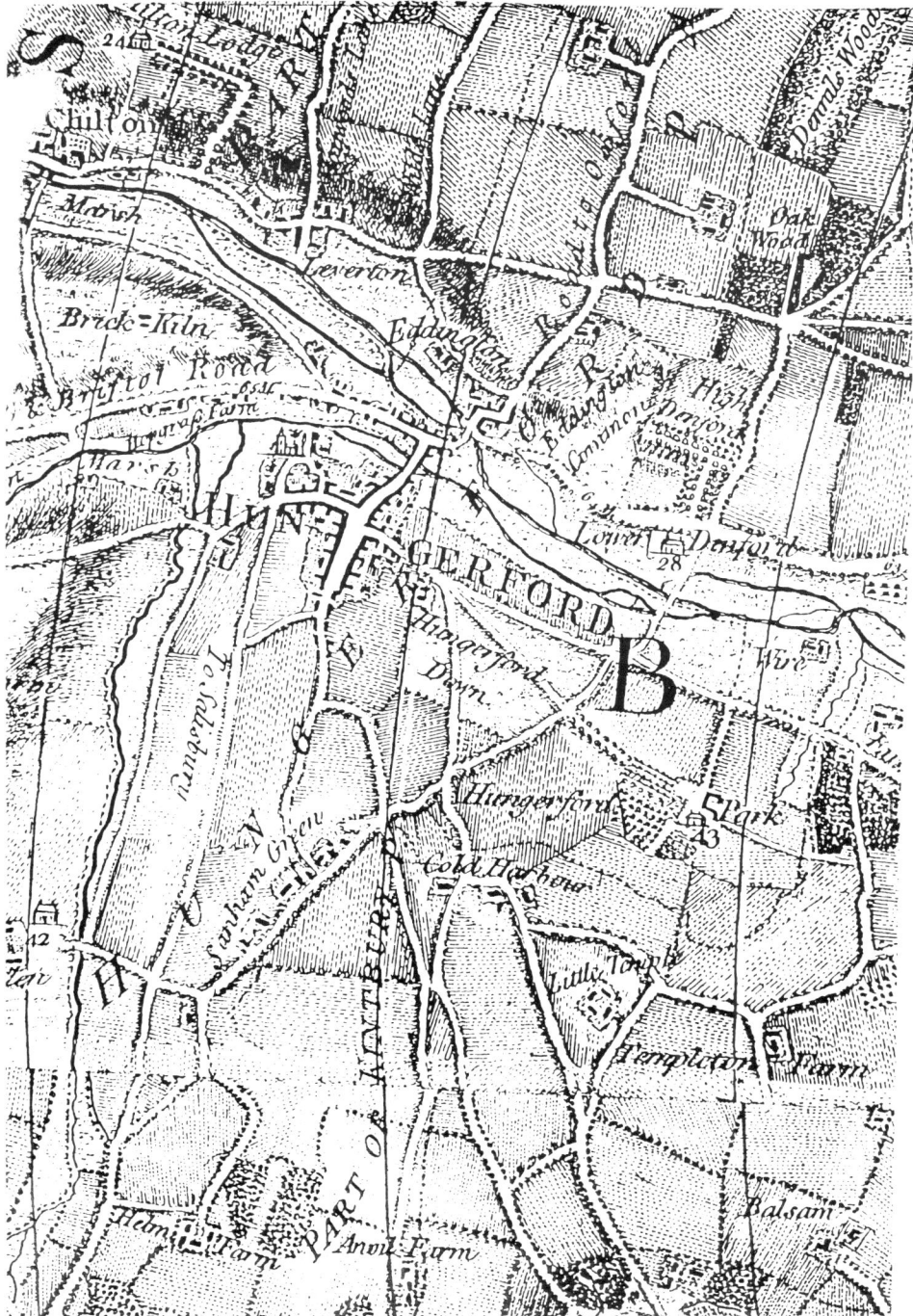

at Calcot,which was held by the Priory at Noyon,were dispossessed by Alan de Fernham who held from the Prior,so that he could give it to his son—in—law.The Feet of Fine indicate a constant stream of land disputes as men sought to define or extend their holdings.In 1281 Roger de Inkepenn went to court about 1 messuage,3 carucates and 1 virgate in Ingepenn and Hampstead Mareschal together with 40s rent in Cherleton,co. Wilts.He was allowed to retain them.In 1310 Philip le Deyer was in court as plaintiff over 2 messuages and 2 acres of land in Hungerford and Sandon,co Berks.and 1 messuage,3 1/2 acres of land and the moiety of 1 acre of meadow in Cherleton by Hungerford co.Wilts.The plaintiff held in consideration of 20 marks.1 mark = 6s 8d.

Further up the scale were the small landowners.Many of them locally were quite successful and gave their names to their properties.John Homedieu who was mentioned as paying 11 1/2d in the 1332 Tax list held Undewe's or Undy's Farm from Roger de Stitchcombe.Roger held Charlton and gave land opposite the mill at Eddington to extend the weir.Sir Steven de Hanville and his lady owned Godingeflod in the 13th century,it later became Anvilles.John Belet of Enborne held Englefloed—Belet in 1230,the name altered from Beletsdon to Balsdon or Balsam. He also held 1 hide in Hungerford—Engleford as a quarter of a knight's fee from 1204 — 1208.Templeyngeflod or Templeton had been granted to the Knights Templar in 1147.Hungerford had a Temple St.in 1836,did it lead that way?Robert and Thomas Hoppegras bought land in Charlton in 1332.The 18th century maps pre—date the car,canal and railway and give an insight into the historical appearance of this district.The Marshalls held Hamstead Marshall in the 13th century,it later passed from Maud to her son the Earl of Norfolk.

The contrast between the life of an Earl and one of his dependants was enormous.The Earl moved his retinue about the country,often the Countess did not accompany him,though she was not withdrawn from public life.On the contrary,political manouevring required much entertaining at one of their larger homes.A castle might be made relatively comfortable with glass in the windows and carpets on the floor,with painted wall hangings or wainscoting to offset the cold of the stone.There was very little furniture,the principle item being the lord's bed which was dismantled to load onto the pack horses for journeys.The tables were all trestles,and all but the lord and lady sat on benches,not chairs,to eat.Most people in the castle stood for long periods or sat on the floor and they slept on palliasses on the benches or in the rushes on the floor.

Earl Simon's travels took him not only round England but also to France at the King's directive.He undertook many missions, and by 1258 when the barons had come into confrontation with the king he was regarded as the most prominent man in the kingdom.After the king's defeat and capture,Earl Simon ruled England until his death at the Battle of Evesham in 1265.His lands passed to the Crown and thence to Prince Edmund — "Crouchback" who became Earl of Leicester and Lancaster.

Chapter Eight

A Possible Chronology and Pattern of Settlement

With reference to the preceding chapters a possible chronology
can be estimated for the foundation of Hungerford.

The very earliest Saxon settlements in the sixth century were in
river valleys,often at fords.Archaeological evidence has been
found proving a sixth century Saxon presence at Undy's Farm.It is
quite conceivable that this settlement could have included
scattered houses at,or near,the ford.The climate became wetter
and it became difficult to sustain a viable settlement in the
valley bottom.But the river crossing place came to be known as
the "hunger" ford.

Later settlements were established along the slopes of the
Kennet,Shalbourn and Inge valleys.One manor came to be called
Inglefol,probably because it had once looked to Ingepenne as the
lords' central hall.Inglefol enclosed two manors,one along the
south side of the Kennet,the other along the east side of the
Shalbourne stream.The ford into this manor was still known as the
"hunger" ford to distinguish it from "den" ford.

By 1142 under the Earls of Leicester a new market town had been
created at the "hunger" ford,to be in the best position for trade
and communications.This was only possible because the Earl owned
Inglefol and had jurisdiction over all the land involved.

The jurisdiction of the town of Hungerford included that of the
manor of Inglefol.Successive references to the manor of
Hungerford-Engleford(VCHBerks.) can be seen in the centuries
following.

This explains why the charter in the time of King James I granted
the Town AND Manor of Hungerford to the trustees who became
collectively the lords of this manor.

Bibliography

Adams,W.M.   Sylvan Savernake & Its Story   (c.1910)
Bennett,H.S.   Life on the English Manor 1150-1400   (1937)
Bettey,J.H.   The Landscape of Wessex
Bright,J.W.   West Saxon Gospels   (1904-6)
Chibnall,M.   Anglo-Norman England 1066-1166 (1986)
Crawford,O.G.S.   Anglo Saxon Bounds of Bedwyn & Burbage
DeGray Birch,W   Cartularium Saxonicum   (1885-1893)
Dodgshon & Butler eds. Historical Geography of England & Wales
Douglas & Greenway eds.English Historical Documents 1042-1189
Ekwall,E.   The Concise Dictionary of English Placenames
Fry,E.A.   Calendar of Wilts.Feet of Fine 1195 - 1272
Garmonsway,G.N.   Anglo Saxon Chronicle   (1953)
Gelling,Dr.M.   Place-Names of Berkshire,vols.2 & 3   (1976)
Gelling,Dr.M.   Signposts to The Past   (1988)
Gelling,Dr.M.   unpublished letter to the author   (1991)
Hidden,N.   The Manor of Hidden
Labarge,M.W.   A Baronial Household of the 13th Cent.(1965)
Lysons,S.& D.   Magna Britannia Berkshire   (1806)
Margary,Dr.I.   Roman Roads In Britain   (1955)
Morris,J.   ed.   Domesday Book;Berks.and Wilts. Phillimore.
Morris,R.   Churches In The Landscape   (1989)
Platt,C.   The English Medieval Town   (1976)
Pugh,   Abstract of Feet of Fine,Wilts 1272 -1327
Round,J.H.   Feudal England   (1895)
Stenton,Sir F.   Anglo-Saxon England   (3rd edn 1971)
Stevenson,J.   Chronicon Monasterii Abingdon(1858)
Summers,Rev.W.H.   The Story of Hungerford in Berkshire
Thorpe,B.   Diplomatorium Anglicum Aevi Saxonicum(1865)
TVAS--Ford,S   TVAS Interim Report   (1989)
VCH Berks.   Victoria County History,Berkshire
WAM.   Wilts.Archaeological & Natural History Society Magazine
Whitelock,D.   The Beginnings of English Society (1952)